COUNTRY BEAR'S NEIGHBOUR

COUNTRY BEAR'S NEIGHBOUR

Larry Dane Brimner

Pictures by
Ruth Tietjen Councell

ORCHARD BOOKS

LONDON

Text copyright © 1988 by Larry Dane Brimner
Illustrations copyright © 1988 by Ruth Tietjen Councell
Originally published in the United States in 1988
by Orchard Books
First published in Great Britain in 1988 by
ORCHARD BOOKS
10 Golden Square, London W1R 3AF
Orchard Books Australia
14 Mars Road, Lane Cove, NSW 2066
1 85213 122 5
Printed in Hong Kong by Wing King Tong

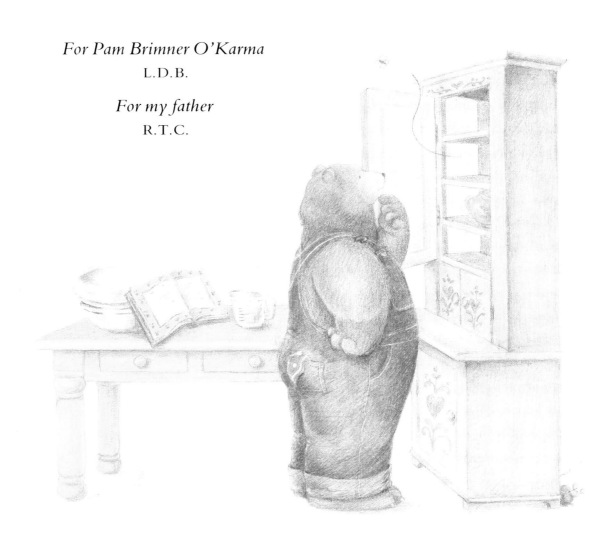

For Pam Brimner O'Karma
L.D.B.

For my father
R.T.C.

Good morning, Country Bear.
What's in that bowl?

You want to borrow some apples?
Certainly!
That's what neighbours are for.

Hullo, Country Bear, have you come to see me again?

Oh.
You thought you had some sugar,
but you can't find any.
I'll get some, Country Bear.
That's what neighbours are for.

Back again, Country Bear?
An egg?

Yes, Country Bear.
I think I can find you an egg.

Now what, Country Bear?
Flour and walnuts?
Cinnamon and butter?

Is there anything else?

You are lucky
I am a good neighbour,
Country Bear.

Absolutely not!
Don't even ask, Country Bear!
You have my apples,
my sugar,
my flour,
my walnuts
my cinnamon,
the butter,
the milk,
AND
the only egg.

Oh?
For me?
Why, Country Bear.
Thank you.

Now come and share it with me.
That's what neighbours are for.

Country Bear's Apple and Walnut Cake

500 g/ 1½ lbs eating apples,
   peeled and thinly sliced
100 g/ 4 oz granulated sugar
1 teaspoon cinnamon
50 g/ 2 oz chopped walnuts
100 g/ 4 oz plain flour
175 g/ 6 oz castor sugar

¾ teaspoon baking powder
¼ teaspoon salt
1 egg, well beaten
3 teaspoons water
4 tablespoons evaporated milk
6 tablespoons melted butter,
   cooled

You will also need:

1 deep 9-inch (23-cm) round
   baking dish
2 mixing bowls
1 whisk
1 wooden spoon

Preheat oven to 160°C (325°F or Gas
Mark 3)

Well butter the baking dish and place in the
apples. Sprinkle the granulated sugar and
cinnamon over the apples. Next sprinkle the
walnuts over the apples.

In a mixing bowl, sift together the flour, the
sugar, baking powder and salt. Set it aside. In
the second bowl whisk together the egg, water,
evaporated milk and melted butter.

Add the egg mixture all at once to the flour
mixture. Stir with the wooden spoon until
smooth. Pour the batter over the apples. Bake
for about 1 hour or until golden.

Enjoy Country Bear's apple and walnut cake
with a friend.